THE ROAD

Cormac McCarthy

AUTHORED by Kalliope Dalto
UPDATED AND REVISED by Michelle Rosenberg

COVER DESIGN by Table XI Partners LLC
COVER PHOTO by Olivia Verma and © 2005 GradeSaver, LLC

BOOK DESIGN by Table XI Partners LLC

Published by GradeSaver LLC, www.gradesaver.com

First published in the United States of America by GradeSaver LLC. 2013

ISBN 978-1-60259-398-5

Printed in the United States of America

For other products and additional information please visit http://www.gradesaver.com

Table of Contents

Table of Contents

Table of Contents

Table of Contents

Teaching Guide - About the Author

Cormac McCarthy's works revel in the shadows of human nature, but McCarthy himself had a remarkably conventional childhood. He was born Charles Joseph McCarthy in Providence, Rhode Island, on July 20, 1933. He later changed his name to Cormac, meaning "son of Charles," to honor his father.

His family moved to Knoxville, Tennessee, in 1937. His father, a lawyer, took a job with the Tennessee Valley Authority legal staff, and remained with the TVA for the next thirty years. Although his childhood biography lacks any particularly traumatic or violent events, a number of key themes in McCarthy's works--travel, the human affinity for bloodshed, and father-son relationships--are rooted in his formative experiences.

McCarthy grew up in the Catholic church, attended Catholic high school, and enrolled at the University of Tennessee in 1951. He completed only one year, however, before deciding to enlist in the U.S. Air Force. He served four years in the military before returning to the University of Tennessee in 1957, where he found himself slowly gravitating towards fiction writing. After publishing two stories in the campus literary magazine The Phoenix, he won Ingram-Merrill Foundation grants for creative writing in both 1959 and 1960. Convinced of his potential for success, he left the university in 1960 to pursue his writing career.

McCarthy moved to Chicago and became an auto mechanic to support himself while he worked on his first novel. He married Lee Holleman, with whom he had one son, Cullen McCarthy. Soon afterward, the couple returned to Tennessee, but the marriage dissolved. Such personal troubles seem not to have distracted him from his work, however. In 1965, McCarthy published his debut novel, *The Orchard Keeper*, which won the William Faulkner Award.

McCarthy has enjoyed sustained critical success since his debut. In 1965, he won an American Academy of Arts and Letters traveling fellowship. This and a later Rockefeller Foundation grant allowed him to travel Europe, where he met and married Ann DeLisle. They eventually settled in Ibiza, a Spanish island, so that McCarthy could finish revising his second novel, *Outer Dark.*

McCarthy continued to win prestigious awards and publish work throughout the 60's, including the novel *Child of God* and the screenplay for the PBS film *The Gardeners's Son*. In 1976, he separated from DeLisle and moved to El Paso, Texas. One of his most acclaimed books, *Suttree*, was published in 1979, the culmination of more than 20 years of work. McCarthy was awarded the prestigious MacArthur Fellowship. With the 1985 publication of *Blood Meridian*, his work began to gain mainstream attention. Declared one of the best novels of the twentieth century by critic Harold Bloom, *Blood Meridian* perhaps best captures the bleak cynicism at the core of McCarthy's body of work.

One of McCarthy's better-known novels is the first novel of his so-called Border Trilogy, *All the Pretty Horses*. This novel also features characters who swirl in the maelstrom of unforeseen, inescapable evil. Despite its bleak themes, the book built upon the acclaim of *Blood Meridian*, meeting with both critical attention and commercial success in 1992. In addition to remaining a New York Times bestseller for six months, it won the National Book Award and National Book Critics Circle Award.

In recent years, McCarthy's acclaim has expanded to include Hollywood films. His two most recent works, *No Country for Old Men* (2005) and *The Road* (2006), have seen great success in their film adaptations. In 2008, McCarthy received the PEN/Saul Bellow Award for Achievement in American Fiction. He currently lives near Santa Fe with his third wife Jennifer and their son. He spends his free time as a research fellow at the Santa Fe Institute.

Teaching Guide - Study Objectives

If all of the elements of this lesson plan are employed, students will develop the following powers, skills, and understanding:

1. To gain an understanding of the underlying themes of *The Road* and how these fit into the tradition of apocalyptic fiction.

2. To trace the development of the lead characters and examine the morality of their decisions.

3. To understand how the author's unique literary style shapes the text.

4. To analyze the symbols and motifs integral to *The Road*.

Teaching Guide - Common Core Standards

- 9-10 - CCSS.ELA-Literacy.CCRA.R.4 Interpret words and phrases as they are used in a text, including determining technical, connotative, and figurative meanings, and analyze how specific word choices shape meaning or tone.

- 9-10 - CCSS.ELA-Literacy.CCRA.R.5 Analyze the structure of texts, including how specific sentences, paragraphs, and larger portions of the text (e.g., a section, chapter, scene, or stanza) relate to each other and the whole.

- 9-10 - CCSS.ELA-Literacy.CCRA.R.7 Integrate and evaluate content presented in diverse media and formats, including visually and quantitatively, as well as in words.

- 9-10 - CCSS.ELA-Literacy.CCRA.R.2 Determine central ideas or themes of a text and analyze their development; summarize the key supporting details and ideas.

- 9-10 - CCSS.ELA-Literacy.CCRA.R.9 Analyze how two or more texts address similar themes or topics in order to build knowledge or to compare the approaches the authors take.

- 9-10 - CCSS.ELA-Literacy.CCRA.R.6 Assess how point of view or purpose shapes the content and style of a text.

- 9-10 - CCSS.ELA-Literacy.CCRA.R.2 Determine central ideas or themes of a text and analyze their development; summarize the key supporting details and ideas.

Teaching Guide - Introduction to The Road

Cormac McCarthy's career in literature has been long and varied, but it was *The Road*, his first foray into apocalyptic storytelling, that earned him international acclaim and the 2007 Pulitzer Prize for Fiction. The novel's bleak future and everyman protagonist have inspired near-universal praise from critics, academics and the general reading public. Many readers are captivated by the bond between "the man" and "the boy" who serve as the novel's nameless heroes and fight to keep their lives and values intact. McCarthy says that the book was inspired by a trip to Texas with his young son; some of the conversations between the book's protagonists are based on real exchanges from that journey.

Key Aspects of The Road

Tone

The Road is extremely somber in tone. The narrative wavers between poetic, awestruck description (especially of dreams or landscapes) and terse, practical action and dialogue. It is almost never lighthearted, though it quite often draws attention to the beauty that can be found in destruction.

Setting

The Road is set in the United States, several years after an unspecified catastrophe (or series of catastrophes) has left the world a burned-out wasteland. There is no government, no infrastructure, no communication system and no food. Brutal cannibal armies wander the country murdering, raping and devouring anyone they encounter. The environment is no longer suitable for most animal life.

Point of View

The story is told in the third-person. The reader sometimes gets insight into the thoughts of the man and, towards the novel's conclusion, the boy.

Character Development

In many ways, *The Road* is a coming-of-age story about the boy, who gradually gains independence and loses some of his naivete. The boy begins the story helpless, scared, and idealistic, extremely reliant on the physical and emotional protection that his father offers. As they travel, the boy becomes more critical of the man's ethical decisions. He also begins to lose faith in finding a better world and other "good guys" to befriend. But despite his disillusionment, it is ultimately the boy's qualities of empathy and faith in others that bear fruit. The hardships that the boy faces make him stronger and better equipped to survive.

The man has a similar arc of disillusionment, but unlike the boy, it saps his strength. As the man loses hope, he becomes both ethically and physically weaker. The values and ideals to which he has taught his son to aspire, remembered from the pre-apocalyptic world, have lost much of their relevance to him. The man never stops fighting for his son, but eventually stops fighting for himself.

Themes

The Journey: Like so many fictional heroes before them, the man and the boy are on a heroic quest for a better life. There is a hoped-for land of plenty at the end of the road, although it is unclear whether either character actually believes this place exists, or if it is just a tool to give their lives some direction.

Morality: The man and the boy constantly have their values put to the test. They struggle to balance their pre-apocalyptic values with the necessities of survival. Sometimes, they are forced to compromise or violate their principles in order to protect each other.

The Father/Son Relationship: The relationship between father and son changes subtly throughout their journey, but remains a cornerstone of the narrative. Their mutual love and protectiveness are essential to their survival. Throughout the text, the man says that, were his son to die, he would follow him, and that the boy "was all that stood between him and death."

Faith: Faith appears in *The Road* in many forms. There is religious imagery throughout (such as the encounter with the mysterious vagrant Ely). There is also the faith that the man encourages the boy to have: that there are other "good guys," that they will not die, that the ocean will be blue and beautiful, that their lives will improve. This faith keeps the boy's spirits up, despite his eventual disillusionment with the ocean. In the end, the boy's faith in other people is rewarded: the first man he encounters after his father's death is a kind protector who provides a safe (and presumably happy) home for the boy.

Symbols

The Fire: The man tells his son that they are "carrying the fire," which represents their adherence to the old values of righteousness and goodness. Because "the fire" is not something physical, it is the one hope that can never disappoint the boy. As long as he remains true, he will always be able to carry the fire, which gives him purpose. Additionally, in a world without electricity or mechanization, fire in the greatest source of power.

The Road: The road itself is a symbol both of the heroes' journey, and of the fall of human civilization. The road is all that remains of civilization:it was constructed long before the apocalypse, and still serves much the same purpose it always has. It is a route for any kind of traveler.

The Ocean: A symbol of unattainable ideals. The man tells stories of the ocean in order to keep up morale and givc his son something to hope for. When they arrive, however, the ocean is not blue: it is grey, cold and dangerous. It is their arrival at the ocean that serves as a point of crucial disillusionment for both characters.

Climax

The Road's climactic scene comes after the two protagonists finally reach the ocean. The boy develops a high fever, and the man stays by his side, caring for him and desperately hoping that he will survive. Ultimately, the boy pulls through, but after this he seems to be stronger and more independent, and the man's spirit seems to be broken for good.

Structure

The book follows the southward journey of the man and the boy along an unnamed road after an apocalyptic event. It tells of the adventures they have, the people they encounter, and their dreams and nightmares.

Teaching Guide - Relationship with Other Books

The Road follows in a long tradition of apocalyptic and post-apocalyptic narratives. Consider other works in this genre, such as *The Handmaid's Tale* or *Oryx and Crake*, by Margaret Atwood, *The Time Machine,* by H.G. Wells, *The Last Book in the Universe*, by Rodman Philbrick, or *The Dog Stars* by Peter Heller.

Also consider other books about quests and journeys. One of the most recognizable works in the genre is *The Odyssey* by Homer. Others include Jack Kerouac's *On the Road* or J.R.R. Tolkien's *The Hobbit.* For insight into the genre and its tropes, consider *The Hero with a Thousand Faces* by Joseph Campbell.

Teaching Guide - Bringing In Technology

Some of suggested projects in this lesson plan have a presentation component, which students can use to showcase their research and interpretation of the text. This could be in the form of a powerpoint presentation, a short film or an infographic. Some classroom activities and homework assignments will require students to use the internet for research. The instructor should advise students as to how to distinguish between a legitimate source (for example, a scholarly journal, published interview, news article or university website) and a discreditable one (for example, a forum page or a blog post).

Day 2: Students might write using dictation software, or record an audio or video version of their scene if they struggle with writing.

Day 3: May integrate audio presentation.

Day 4: Students may use Microsoft Excel or other graphing software to organize their thoughts into charts or diagrams.

Day 5: One of the activities will require a way to play a DVD or stream a video.

Teaching Guide - Notes to the Teacher

The thought questions in this lesson plan provide material and ideas that students can use to write short original essays. For the sake of improving the power of expression, teachers should encourage students to write on topics that have been discussed in class, this time in the more formal writing style expected in a literary essay. However, students should never be discouraged from choosing their own topics.

The questions provided for the final paper are most suitable for student essays. Please remember that grading an essay should never depend on a simple checklist of required content.

Author of Lesson Plan and Sources

Kalliope Dalto, author of Lesson Plan. Completed on December 20, 2013, copyright held by GradeSaver.

Updated and revised Michelle Rosenberg December 21, 2013. Copyright held by GradeSaver.

McCarthy, Cormac. The Road. New York: Alfred A. Knopf, 2006.

Related Links

http://www.poetryfoundation.org/poem/173081
"Darkness" by Lord George Gordon Byron The text of a poem with similar themes and some similar language to *The Road*.

http://www.jstor.org/
Journal Storage A digital library of academic papers, invaluable for finding literary criticism on any text.

http://en.wikipedia.org/wiki/List_of_apocalyptic_and_post-apocalyptic_fiction
Wikipedia List of Post-Apocalyptic and Apocalyptic Works A great starting point for those interested in seeking out more stories about the apocalypse.

http://www.history.com/topics/the-end-of-the-world
Major Religions on the End of the World A good place to start if you want to learn more about the apocalypse in various mythological traditions.

Day 1 - Reading Assignment

Students should read pages 1 - 52.

Common Core Objectives

- CCSS.ELA-Literacy.CCRA.R.4 Interpret words and phrases as they are used in a text, including determining technical, connotative, and figurative meanings, and analyze how specific word choices shape meaning or tone.
- CCSS.ELA-Literacy.CCRA.R.5 Analyze the structure of texts, including how specific sentences, paragraphs, and larger portions of the text (e.g., a section, chapter, scene, or stanza) relate to each other and the whole.

Note that it is perfectly fine to expand any day's work into two days depending on the characteristics of the class, particularly if the class will engage in all of the suggested classroom exercises and activities and discuss all of the thought questions.

Content Summary for Teachers

Pages 1 - 52: This section introduces the two protagonists, a father and son known only as "the man" and "the boy." In the aftermath of an apocalyptic event that destroyed civilization and left the land devastated, the man and the boy are traveling south to keep from freezing to death in the winter. We learn of their routine of scavenging, preparing canned meals over a fire, walking, and storytelling. The man tries very hard to keep the boy from seeing the atrocities they stumble across, and works to keep his spirits up despite their circumstances. The man has strange, poetic dreams. He reminisces about his childhood, before the disaster, and takes the boy to visit his childhood home. They travel into the mountains in order to avoid the murderous cannibal gangs that wander the road. They pass a disfigured old man, and the boy wants to help him but the man does not allow it.

Thought Questions (students consider while they read)

1. The man says of his son, “If he is not the word of God, god never spoke." What does this say about his attitude towards the boy? What does it say about his personal belief system?
2. Telling stories is an important part of the relationship between the man and the boy. Why do you think this is?
3. “Can I ask you something? Yes. Of course you can." "What would you do if I died?" If you died I would want to die too." "So you could be with me?" "Yes. So I could be with you." "Okay.”

What do you think about this conversation? For example, do you find it disturbing, touching, necessary? What does it reveal about the two characters?

4. Why do you think the the boy is so scared when they visit his father's childhood home?
5. Why do you think the two protagonists of *The Road* are not given names?

Vocabulary (in order of appearance)

Page 4:

- Alabaster: A pale, white, translucent stone.

Page 6:

- Ratchet: A rotational tool.

Page 7:

- Slutlamp: A bottle of oil with a cloth wick.

Page 14:

- Cauterize: To burn a wound with a heated instrument in order to prevent infection.

Page 15:

- Vestibular: Relating to one's sense of balance.
- Declination: A downward slope.

Page 16:

- Balefire: A bonfire.

Page 18:

- Pipeclayed: Made white.

Page 24:

- Discalced: Barefoot

Page 32:

- Immolate: To kill as a sacrifice, particularly by burning

- Sectarian: One who belongs to a religious sect.

Page 38:

- Lozenge: An object with a diamond-like rhombus shape.

Page 40:

- Morel: A spongy, brown edible mushroom.

Page 48:

- Macadam: A type of pavement composed of compacted layers of broken stone.
- Mastic: A type of paste-like cement used in the construction of highways.

Additional Homework

1. Re-read and annotate any descriptions of dreams that have been described so far in the text. What do you think these dreams might mean? Compose a paragraph analyzing a dream of your choice from this section.

Day 1 - Discussion of Thought Questions

1. The man says of his son, “If he is not the word of God, god never spoke." What does this say about his attitude towards the boy? What does it say about his personal belief system?

   Time: 10 minutes

   Discussion: This quote is an early indication of the pervasive religious aspect of the man’s relationship with the boy. The man's language and behavior at times indicate that he believes his son to has a divine aspect, at least on a symbolic level. The man perceives his son as the last incarnation of purity and innocence, much like Christ is portrayed in Christian religious texts as an innocent lamb. This particular quote may be read as an indication that the boy is all that remains of the man’s faith, and that the boy's existence is the only thing that could still serve as evidence of a greater power.

2. Telling stories is an important part of the relationship between the man and the boy. Why do you think this is?

   Time: 5-7 minutes

   Discussion: As a storyteller, the man tries inspire hope in his son. He tells “old stories of courage and justice as he remember[s] them." These are qualities the boy may never have seen, having grown up in the aftermath of the apocalypse. The man believes it is important for his son to possess a moral code, and in the absence of real heroes to set an example for the boy, he must invent some--the man does this by telling his son stories.

3. “Can I ask you something? Yes. Of course you can." "What would you do if I died?" If you died I would want to die too." "So you could be with me?" "Yes. So I could be with you." "Okay.”

   What do you think about this conversation? For example, do you find it disturbing, touching, necessary? What does it reveal about the two characters?

Time: 7-10 minutes

Discussion:

Students might note that, unfortunately, death is an inescapable reality of the world these two characters live in, and there is no way to avoid discussing it. This conversation is a necessity: it assuages the worries of the boy, whose father is his whole world. It also cements the man's dependence on his son as the reason for his own continued survival.

Another thing to consider is the pressure that this puts on the boy. He knows that he must do everything possible to keep himself alive, or else he will be to blame for his father's death.

4. Why do you think the the boy is so scared when they visit his father's childhood home?

   Time: 5-7 minutes

   Discussion: One possible answer to this question is that to the boy, this house represents a world that he has only known through the happy stories of his father. Being inside the house shows him that world was once real, but is now dead. It is both the confirmation and the destruction of something that had only been a fantasy to the boy. A less speculative answer, however, might be that the boy is scared of what or who might be lurking in the house, waiting to attack (a fear that later is revealed to be a practical one).

5. Why do you think the two protagonists of *The Road* are not given names?

   Time: 5 minutes

Discussion: By referring to them as "the man" and "the boy,' McCarthy allows both to be archetypal everyman figures onto which the reader may easily project him/herself. Additionally, their namelessness highlights the loss of identity the apocalypse has thrust upon them, and the new irrelevance of things that were once highly valued parts of the human experience.

Day 1 - Short Answer Quiz

1. From what perspective is the story told?

2. Who are the book's protagonists?

3. Are the names of the book's protagonists ever mentioned?

4. The characters enter an abandoned house. Whose house was it, and when did they live there?

5. Who is the book's author?

6. Identify one unusual feature of the grammar and punctuation employed in *The Road*.

7. What is the relationship between the two protagonists?

---

8. What does the boy draw on his mask?

---

9. The man calls the boy "the word of ___."

---

10. How do the man and the boy carry their supplies?

Short Answer Quiz Key

1. The story is narrated by a third person limited omniscient narrator.
2. The Man and The Boy.
3. No.
4. The man lived there as a child, before the apocalypse.
5. Cormac McCarthy
6. Possible answers include: lack of punctuation; lack of apostrophes in contractions; creative capitalization; few commas
7. They are father and son.
8. Fangs.
9. God.
10. In a cart.

Day 1 - Crossword Puzzle

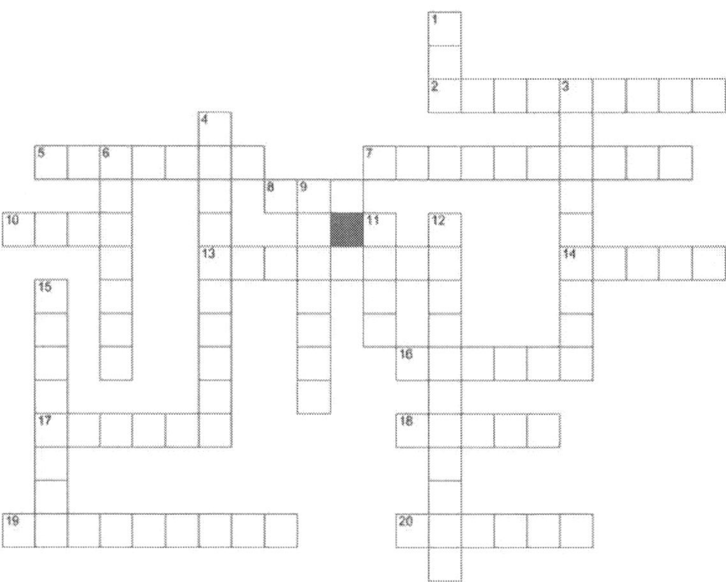

ACROSS

2. Barefoot
5. A rotational tool.
7. Made white.
8. What the sky is filled with.
10. The boy & the man are carrying the _____.
13. To burn oneself alive.
14. The direction in which our heroes are traveling.
16. The man & the boy must get to warmer climes before _____.
17. The man is the boy's ______.
18. The boy draws these on his mask.
19. A follower of a religious sect.
20. The mushrooms the man & the boy snack on.

DOWN

1. "If he is not the word of ______, ______ never spoke."
3. A white, translucent stone.
4. Relating to one's sense of balance.
6. The man & the boy travel along this.
9. How the man entertains the boy.
11. How they carry their supplies.
12. A downward slope.
15. A bonfire.

Crossword Puzzle Answer Key

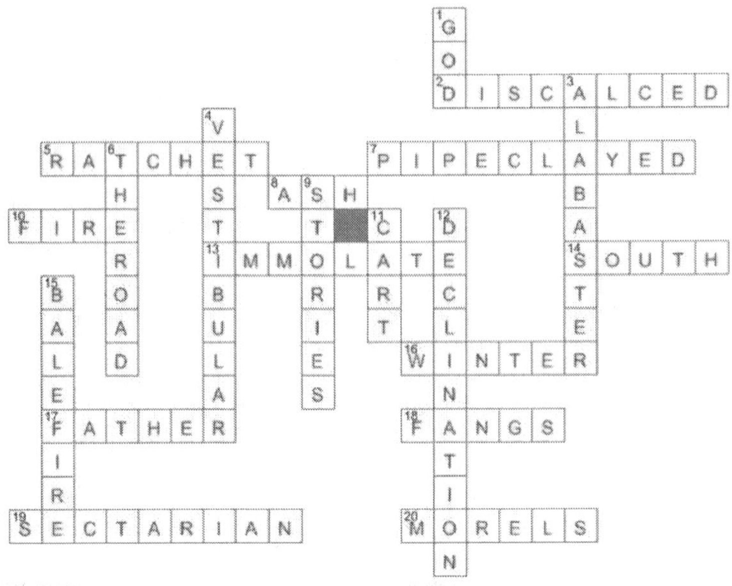

ACROSS

2. Barefoot
5. A rotational tool.
7. Made white.
8. What the sky is filled with.
10. The boy & the man are carrying the ____.
13. To burn oneself alive.
14. The direction in which our heroes are traveling.
16. The man & the boy must get to warmer climes before ____.
17. The man is the boy's ______.
18. The boy draws these on his mask.
19. A follower of a religious sect.
20. The mushrooms the man & the boy snack on.

DOWN

1. "If he is not the word of ______, ______ never spoke."
3. A white, translucent stone.
4. Relating to one's sense of balance.
6. The man & the boy travel along this.
9. How the man entertains the boy.
11. How they carry their supplies.
12. A downward slope.
15. A bonfire.

Day 1 - Vocabulary Quiz

Terms

1. ____ Alabaster
2. ____ Ratchet
3. ____ Slutlamp
4. ____ Cauterize
5. ____ Vestibular
6. ____ Declination
7. ____ Balefire
8. ____ Pipeclayed
9. ____ Discalced
10. ____ Immolate
11. ____ Sectarian
12. ____ Lozenge
13. ____ Morel
14. ____ Macadam
15. ____ Mastic

Answers

A. One who belongs to a religious sect.
B. To kill as a sacrifice, particularly by burning
C. A downward slope.
D. Relating to one's sense of balance.
E. A bottle of oil with a cloth wick.
F. An object with a diamond-like rhombus shape.
G. To burn a wound with a heated instrument in order to prevent infection.
H. Made white.
I. A pale, white, translucent stone.
J. A type of pavement composed of compacted layers of broken stone.
K. A spongy, brown edible mushroom.
L. A type of paste-like cement used in the construction of highways.
M. A rotational tool.
N. A bonfire.
O. Barefoot.

Vocabulary Quiz Answer Key

1. I
2. M
3. E
4. G
5. D
6. C
7. N
8. H
9. O
10. B
11. A
12. F
13. K
14. J
15. L

Day 1 - Classroom Activities

1. Cormac McCarthy's Language

Kind of Activity: Classwide Discussion
Objective: To recognize McCarthy's unique stylistic choices and analyze their significance in the narrative.
Common Core State Standards: CCSS.ELA-Literacy.CCRA.R.4; CCSS.ELA-Literacy.CCRA.R.5
Time: 30 minutes

Structure:

Discuss McCarthy's language choices with the class. Ask what they have noticed about his dialogue and his descriptions. Draw students' attention to the way the narrative changes between flowery, poetic description (especially of dreams or landscapes) and terse, practical action and dialogue.

Some questions to guide discussion include:

- Is the contrast in writing styles jarring?

- Why do you think the author chose to use long, flowery sentences and obscure words?

- What purpose do the short sentences and simple words serve?

- Do you feel that one type of description (elaborate and flowery vs terse and practical) is more powerful or effective than the other? Why or why not?

Next, have students work individually to select three long, florid descriptions and three short, simple ones from the text you have covered so far. Have each student read their chosen passages aloud and explain why that particular part stood out to them. If multiple students have chosen the same passage, discuss their perspectives and how they differ. This activity should make the contrasts in McCarthy's writing more recognizable to students.

As a class, discuss patterns that emerge throughout the text: for instance, the use of short, vague sentences in dialogue and more elaborate sentences in dream sequences.

Ideans for Differentiated Instruction:

-Provide textual examples to illustrate the stylistic differences, in case some students have trouble differentiating.

-Encourage students to read passages aloud to each other if it helps them to identify stylistic differences.

-Be cognizant of fluency levels and comfort with public speaking when asking students to read aloud.

Assessment Ideas:

-Students should be able to select three long, florid descriptions and three short, simple ones from the text you have covered so far.

-Have students write and submit a paragraph about why they chose their passage, what stylistic choices they have identified within it, and why those choices might have been made.

2. Dialogue in *The Road*

Kind of Activity: Role Play
Objective: To recognize the use of the simple, direct style of dialogue employed in the novel.
Common Core State Standards: CCSS.ELA-Literacy.RL.9-10.4, CCSS.ELA-Literacy.CCRA.R.5, CCSS.ELA-Literacy.CCRA.R.4
Time: 40 minutes

Structure:

As a class, identify the unique attributes of the dialogue found in the novel. The dialogue in *The Road* tends to occur in blocks, without quotation marks and with infrequent apostrophes. Because of this, students may occasionally have trouble identifying who the speaker is.

Assign students to form groups of two, and have each group select a section of dialogue between the man and the boy to read aloud. One student should read the part of the boy and the other should read the part of the man. After each pair has read their section of dialogue aloud, ask for volunteers to perform their section for the class. Hearing the dialogue read aloud should clarify some of the confusion that students may have had over the identity of the speaker. Ask the class if they have any questions that were not cleared up by hearing it aloud.

Once several pairs have performed for the class, ask students how they would describe the dialogue found throughout the novel. Some points for discussion include:

-What words or phrases are repeated often by the characters, and in what context do they appear? (For example, the boy's use of the word "okay."

-How does the dialogue compare to McCarthy's elaborate, florid sentences of narration and description? Which style conveys more information?

-Are there significant stylistic differences between the speech patterns of the man and the boy? If so, what are they? If not, how can the reader distinguish between the two characters?

Ideans for Differentiated Instruction:

-More theatrically inclined students may be called upon to perform the dialogues for the class.

-Group students of different skill levels together, so that advanced students may assist those who struggle.

-Assign passages based on students' skill levels, providing more challenging work to those who are ready for it.

Assessment Ideas:

-Have students select a recurrent phrase from the novel's dialogue and write a paragraph explaining its significance.

-Have one student in each group act as a scribe, taking down notes on any student responses or discussions that happen within the group.

Day 2 - Reading Assignment

Students should read pages 52 - 115.

Common Core Objectives

- CCSS.ELA-Literacy.CCRA.R.7 Integrate and evaluate content presented in diverse media and formats, including visually and quantitatively, as well as in words.
- CCSS.ELA-Literacy.CCRA.R.2 Determine central ideas or themes of a text and analyze their development; summarize the key supporting details and ideas.
- CCSS.ELA-Literacy.CCRA.R.9 Analyze how two or more texts address similar themes or topics in order to build knowledge or to compare the approaches the authors take.
- CCSS.ELA-Literacy.CCRA.R.6 Assess how point of view or purpose shapes the content and style of a text.
- CCSS.ELA-Literacy.CCRA.L.2 Demonstrate command of the conventions of standard English capitalization, punctuation, and spelling when writing.
- CCSS.ELA-Literacy.CCRA.W.3 Write narratives to develop real or imagined experiences or events using effective technique, well-chosen details and well-structured event sequences.

Note that it is perfectly fine to expand any day's work into two days depending on the characteristics of the class, particularly if the class will engage in all of the suggested classroom exercises and activities and discuss all of the thought questions.

Content Summary for Teachers

Pages 52 - 115:

The man recalls the apocalyptic event and its immediate aftermath. During the destruction of the cities, the man's wife gave birth to their son. As time passed, she became depressed and hopeless, and eventually left her husband and son and committed suicide.

The man and the boy hide from a gang of threatening-looking men. The boy is captured by one of the gang members, but the man shoots the captor in the head and rescues his son. There is now only a single bullet left in the man's pistol. The boy is upset and becomes increasingly depressed, but the man insists that the dead man was a "bad guy." The boy also sees another "little boy" in the woods, and becomes obsessively worried about him.

The two run out of food, and begin to slowly die of starvation. Out of desperation, they enter a grand but ominous old house outside of a town. They find signs of people living there, and the boy is terrified, but the man continues to search for food. However, they discover a cellar full of naked, imprisoned people being held captive by cannibals. The man and the boy flee, but see a group of people approaching the house. They hide in the woods, hoping they won't be discovered.

Thought Questions (students consider while they read)

1. Do you think it is accurate for the man to divide people into "good guys" and "bad guys"? Why might that be problematic, especially in terms of teaching his son how to view the world?
2. Why does the man's wife kill herself?
3. What does it mean that the boy and the man are "carrying the fire"?
4. The man's pistol is loaded with only two bullets. Discuss the significance of the pistol in the text.
5. Why do you think McCarthy chose to make the exact nature of the apocalyptic event so ambiguous?

Vocabulary (in order of appearance)

Page 54:

- Penitent: Remorseful

Page 56:

- Cheroot: A kind of cigar with square, un-tapered ends.

Page 59:

- Meconium: A stool-like substance discharged by a newborn infant.

Page 75:

- Claggy: Gummed up; sticky.

Page 76:

- Quoits: A ring-tossing game.

Page 79:

- Sappers: Military personnel responsible for detecting and disarming mines.

Page 85:

- Viaduct: A series of high arches that support a bridge or overpass.

Page 88:

- Parsible: Able to be understood.

Page 90:

- Viscera: Internal organs; guts.
- Truncheoned: Beaten in with a club or staff.

Page 92:

- Catamite: A young male slave, kept for sexual purposes.

Additional Homework

1. Look at *The Road*'s portrayal of women, especially the man's wife. Write an essay explaining whether or not you find the novel's portrayal of women to be sexist, supporting your opinion with evidence from the text.

Day 2 - Discussion of Thought Questions

1. Do you think it is accurate for the man to divide people into "good guys" and "bad guys"? Why might that be problematic, especially in terms of teaching his son how to view the world?

   Time: 7-10 minutes

   Discussion: This classification is something of a problematic binary. The man creates the false impression that people can only be one thing or the other, all good or all bad. Since he feels he cannot trust anyone he encounters on the road, he must label them as bad guys. Unfortunately, this label can be used to justify any action he may take toward perceived "bad guys." On the one hand, it can be seen as a noble effort to protect his son from guilt over violence done to strangers who are dangerous. One the other hand, it risks damaging his son's capacity to empathize and connect.

2. Why does the man's wife kill herself?

   Time: 5-7 minutes

   Discussion: There are many possible answers to this question. Encourage students to examine the character from different angles, and weigh her possible motivations. Discuss her fear of the dissolution of civilization and her reluctance to see her loved ones die. You may also want to ask how students feel about her decision: was it cowardly? Brave? Practical? Weigh it against the man's decision to try to keep his son alive.

3. What does it mean that the boy and the man are "carrying the fire"?

   Time: 5-7 minutes

   Discussion: "The fire" represents the man's belief in adherence to old values of righteousness and goodness. Because "the fire" is not something physical, it is one hope that can never disappoint the boy. As long as he remains true to the moral codes his father has taught him, the boy will always be able to carry the fire, which gives him a sense of purpose. In a world without electricity or mechanization, fire is not only a fundamental component of survival, but also the greatest source of power.

4. The man's pistol is loaded with only two bullets. Discuss the significance of the pistol in the text.

   Time: 5-7 minutes

   Discussion: The man and the boy regard the pistol with a talismanic reverence. It is the only way they can protect themselves from violent attacks, but its two bullets limit the extent of its protection. It would be of no use in a gunfight or against the cannibalistic gangs. More often than not, the pistol is spoken of as a tool for a quick, painless suicide. The two bullets, so unfit for self-defense, appear perfect for ending the lives of our two heroes. It is interesting to consider which character holds responsibility for the pistol and when: for example, the man always leaves it with the boy whenever he goes exploring alone.

5. Why do you think McCarthy chose to make the exact nature of the apocalyptic event so ambiguous?

   Time: 7-10 minutes

   Discussion: Though McCarthy allows the reader some hints as to why and how civilization has been destroyed, an explicit explanation is never given. It is unlikely that the man even knows exactly what happened, and more importantly, it is irrelevant: his priority is to learn to survive the harsh wasteland of the book's setting and to protect his son. Dwelling on how or why civilization fell does not help him to do this. The unspecified nature of the apocalyptic event also adds a chilling realistic quality to the plot. Were the catastrophe explained, it might be easier for the reader to focus on its fictionalized elements and more difficult to suspend disbelief.

Day 2 - Short Answer Quiz

1. At what time did all the clocks stop?

____

2. Name two activities that the man and the boy do for fun.

____

3. How did the boy's mother die?

____

4. At the beginning of the book, how many bullets are in the pistol?

____

5. How does the man refer to the dangerous people they meet on the road?

____

6. The man and the boy discover some people locked in a basement. Why are they there?

____

7. What are the man and the boy proud to be carrying? (Think metaphorically.)

8. Where are the man and the boy going?

9. Was the boy born before, during, or after the apocalyptic event?

10. How does the man use one of the bullets in the pistol?

Short Answer Quiz Key

1. 1:17
2. They tell stories and play games (Specifying two different types of games is also an acceptable answer.)
3. She killed herself.
4. Two.
5. He calls them the "Bad Guys."
6. They are going to be slaughtered for food.
7. The fire.
8. They are making their way to the south. (Also acceptable: the sea or the ocean.)
9. After. ("During" is also acceptable.)
10. He shoots a man who has captured the boy.

Day 2 - Crossword Puzzle

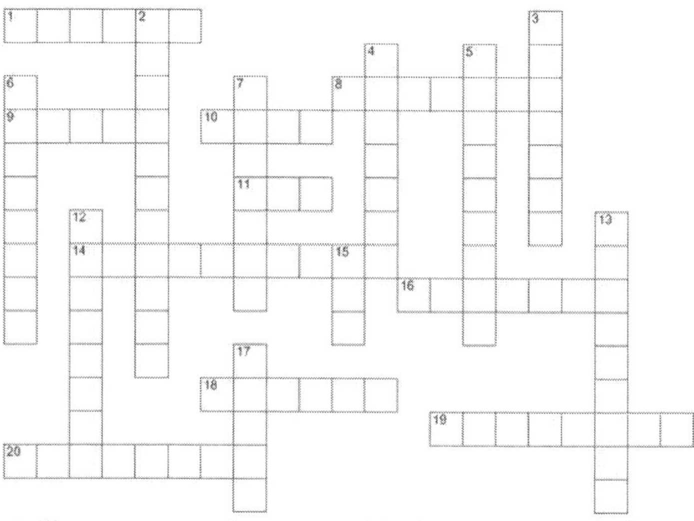

ACROSS

1. A ring-tossing game
8. Military personnel responsible for detecting and disarming mines.
9. The man thinks his son looks like this.
10. The man leaves behind a picture of this person.
11. An animal the boy convinces the man to spare.
14. A name for the cannibal war tribes.
16. A kind of cigar.
18. Gummed up; sticky.
19. Able to be understood or explained.
20. One who feels wishes to be forgiven for past wrongs.

DOWN

2. Beaten in with a club or staff.
3. Internal organs; guts.
4. The man calls their enemies this.
5. Minutes past 1 o'clock at which the clocks stopped.
6. A young male slave.
7. A series of high arches that support a bridge or overpass.
12. The kind of knife the mother kills herself with.
13. The boy is very worried that this person is lost.
15. The number of bullets in the pistol.
17. The boy throws this toy away.

Crossword Puzzle Answer Key

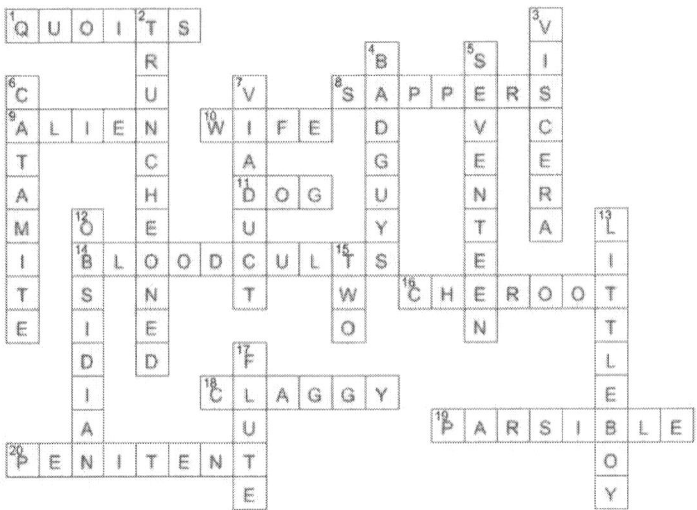

ACROSS

1. A ring-tossing game
8. Military personnel responsible for detecting and disarming mines.
9. The man thinks his son looks like this.
10. The man leaves behind a picture of this person.
11. An animal the boy convinces the man to spare.
14. A name for the cannibal war tribes.
16. A kind of cigar.
18. Gummed up; sticky.
19. Able to be understood or explained.
20. One who feels wishes to be forgiven for past wrongs.

DOWN

2. Beaten in with a club or staff.
3. Internal organs; guts.
4. The man calls their enemies this.
5. Minutes past 1 o'clock at which the clocks stopped.
6. A young male slave.
7. A series of high arches that support a bridge or overpass.
12. The kind of knife the mother kills herself with.
13. The boy is very worried that this person is lost.
15. The number of bullets in the pistol.
17. The boy throws this toy away.

Day 2 - Vocabulary Quiz

Terms	**Answers**
1. ____ Penitent	A. A stool-like substance discharged by a newborn infant.
2. ____ Cheroot	B. Remorseful.
3. ____ Meconium	C. A ring-tossing game.
4. ____ Claggy	D. Able to be understood.
5. ____ Quoits	E. Beaten in with a club or staff.
6. ____ Sappers	F. Gummed up; sticky.
7. ____ Viaduct	G. A series of high arches that support a bridge or overpass.
8. ____ Parsible	H. Internal organs; guts.
9. ____ Viscera	I. Military personnel responsible for detecting and disarming mines.
10. ____ Truncheoned	J. A kind of cigar with square, un-tapered ends.

Vocabulary Quiz Answer Key

1. B
2. J
3. A
4. F
5. C
6. I
7. G
8. D
9. H
10. E

Day 2 - Classroom Activities

1. Did We Cause the Apocalypse?

    Kind of Activity: Creative Writing
    Objective: Examine different explanations for *The Road*'s apocalypse and compare their allegorical significance.
    Common Core State Standards: CCSS.ELA-Literacy.CCRA.R.7; CCSS.ELA-Literacy.CCRA.R.2; CCSS.ELA-Literacy.CCRA.W.3
    Time: 40 minutes

    Structure:

    As a class, discuss the hints we have been given so far about what kind of disaster destroyed civilization. Read through the sections that describe the event, and look for clues as to what may have happened. Take note of the after-effects as well, on both society and the environment.

    Students should be called upon to volunteer details that they remember from the text about the apocalypse. These might include widespread fires, severance of long-distance communication, contaminated food and water, death of animals and wildlife, ash-filled sky and air, etc.

    Ask students whether they feel humanity is implied to be directly responsible for the cataclysm (such as in a nuclear disaster), or indirectly responsible (such as not adequately taking care of the environment). This may open up into a discussion of how often the concept of the apocalypse is used as a punishment for mankind's transgressions. Do students feel that this applies to *The Road*? Discuss how the exact nature of the apocalypse and mankind's role in it might affect the message of the book.

    Assign students to individually compose a short story describing the apocalyptic event that brought about the circumstances in which *The Road* is set. Students should take care to incorporate details from the text regarding the nature of the event, and try to explain some or all of the after-effects the class has discussed. Most importantly, stories should answer the question of mankind's responsibility for the disaster. Is it a natural consequence of mankind's carelessness? Is it a divine punishment for society's sins? Is it an environmental parable or a morality tale? By writing a story in which the apocalypse is explained, students have a chance to express what they interpret the message of *The Road* to be.

    Ideans for Differentiated Instruction:

    -Review examples of possible catastrophic events, such as a nuclear explosion, a volcanic eruption, or a meteor colliding with the earth.

-For struggling students, provide accounts of catastrophic events (such as first-hand descriptions of nuclear incidents or large-scale hurricanes and flooding). These accounts might be written, audio, or visual.

-More advanced students may wish to write their story in imitation of McCarthy's writing style, as if it were a missing chapter.

Assessment Ideas:

-Have students submit their short stories for review by the instructor.

-Ask students to share parts of their stories aloud and answer questions about their ideas and choices.

2. The Woman and the Boy

Kind of Activity: Creative Writing
Objective: Analyze the character of the boy's mother and the role of women in *The Road.*
Common Core State Standards: CCSS.ELA-Literacy.CCRA.L.2; CCSS.ELA-Literacy.CCRA.R.6; CCSS.ELA-Literacy.CCRA.W.3
Time: 40 minutes

Structure:

Begin by asking the students how they feel about the female characters in the novel. Introduce the idea that many have criticized *The Road* for its portrayal of women: there are very few female characters, and of those few, only the boy's mother is a remotely fleshed-out character. Even she has been criticized as being cold, poorly developed and unsympathetic.

This is a good way to open a general discussion of the book's treatment of the man's wife. Questions for discussion include:

-Why did she kill herself?

-What is the effect of having her written out of the story so early on?

-Were her actions cowardly, especially in comparison to those of the man?

-What do you think about the woman's use of derogatory sexual language about herself? (She calls herself a "faithless slut" in reference to her decision to commit suicide).

-Why is the boy is so detached from the news of her death/disappearance, but so concerned about strangers that they meet?

Ask the class to identify any women mentioned in the novel: who they are, and what the reader knows about them. You might notice that they are all pregnant and/or enslaved. Does this bother the students? How does it affect their experience of the novel?

Once you have wrapped up your class discussion, assign students to individually write a scene with the following premise: what if the novel followed the boy and his mother, instead of the boy and his father? Encourage students to try to keep the mother's character consistent, but give her a more complex and sympathetic role to play. What might this new role change about the book's message? How might the fundamentals of the story change?

Ideans for Differentiated Instruction:

-Students might write using dictation software, or record an audio or video version of their scene if they struggle with writing.

-More advanced students might research feminist scholarship regarding *The Road* and/or Cormac McCarthy's other works.

Assessment Ideas:

-Have students turn in their scenes for evaluation by the instructor.

-During the class discussion, evaluate students' contributions, which should reflect their level of understanding of both the text and the issues being discussed.

Day 3 - Reading Assignment

Students should read page 115 - 174.

Common Core Objectives

- CCSS.ELA-Literacy.CCRA.R.7 Integrate and evaluate content presented in diverse media and formats, including visually and quantitatively, as well as in words.
- CCSS.ELA-Literacy.CCRA.R.9 Analyze how two or more texts address similar themes or topics in order to build knowledge or to compare the approaches the authors take.
- CCSS.ELA-Literacy.CCRA.W.10 Write routinely over extended time frames (time for research, reflection, and revision) and shorter time frames (a single sitting or a day or two) for a range of tasks, purposes, and audiences.
- CCSS.ELA-Literacy.CCRA.L.5 Demonstrate understanding of figurative language, word relationships, and nuances in word meanings.

Note that it is perfectly fine to expand any day's work into two days depending on the characteristics of the class, particularly if the class will engage in all of the suggested classroom exercises and activities and discuss all of the thought questions.

Content Summary for Teachers

Pages 115 - 174:

The man discovers another farmhouse. He is especially cautious after their last experience, but knows they must find food to stay alive. They find some apples and a drink mix, and then continue on their way. The man is terrified that his son will die of starvation.

Fortunately they soon come across yet another farmhouse, this one with a fully stocked disaster shelter. The man and the boy spend a few happy days there, enjoying the luxury of food, running water, and other conveniences. But staying in one place is dangerous and soon they must leave the comfort of the shelter. Bathed, shaved and laden with new provisions, they set out again.

They encounter a strange traveler on the road, an ancient, starving, sickly man who calls himself Ely. The man does not trust him, but the boy feels sorry for him and insists they give him food. Ely has some cryptic and ominous things to say about the mystery of his own survival and the world's apparent abandonment of religion. The next morning, the man insists that they leave Ely behind and travel on, although the boy is upset by this.

Thought Questions (students consider while they read)

1. The man makes comparisons to aliens on two occasions. First he says, "The boy's candlecolored skin was all but translucent. With his great staring eyes he'd the look of an alien." Later, he posits that he himself must appear alien to his son. How could the boy be an alien to his father? How could the man be an alien to his son?
2. When the man finds the abandoned bunker filled with food, why does he tell his son that it belonged to the "good guys"?
3. Overall, do you think the man tries to encourage or discourage his son to hope? Which does he do more? Is this a contradiction?
4. Why do you think the boy throws his flute away?
5. Who do you think Ely is, and why is he included in the story?

Vocabulary (in order of appearance)

Page 116:

- Chary: Cautious, or wary.

Page 117:

- Duff: Decaying organic matter on a forest floor.

Page 121:

- Trellis: A framework on which climbing plants may grow.
- Mudroom: A small room adjacent to a home's entrance where people may leave their coat and shoes.

Page 130:

- Intestate: Without a will.

Page 136:

- Gelid: Very cold.

Page 142:

- Krugerrand: A South African gold coin.

Page 152:

- Sumptuous: Luxurious; rich.

Page 159:

- Scrim: A semi-transparent screen.

Page 168:

- Bivouac: To set up temporary camp in an unsheltered area.

Additional Homework

1. Why do you think Ely calls himself "Ely"? Research the origins of the name, and then write a short possible backstory for the character.

Day 3 - Discussion of Thought Questions

1. The man makes comparisons to aliens on two occasions. First he says, "The boy's candlecolored skin was all but translucent. With his great staring eyes he'd the look of an alien." Later, he posits that he himself must appear alien to his son. How could the boy be an alien to his father? How could the man be an alien to his son?

   Time: 7-10 minutes

   Discussion: Though the first comparison is based on a physical description, it can also be seen as an indication of the man's difficulty understanding and communicating with his son. The boy was born as society was collapsing, and he grew up surrounded by hunger, death, and the harsh necessities of survival. His childhood is almost incomparable to that of the man, who lived most of his life before the apocalypse.

2. When the man finds the abandoned bunker filled with food, why does he tell his son that it belonged to the "good guys"?

   Time: 5-7 minutes

   Discussion: In absence the absence of real heroes and "good guys" for the boy to look up to, the man feels he must fictionalize some. He wants his son to believe in the kindness and generosity of others, but since it is never safe to trust the real people they may encounter, the only people deemed "good guys" are the romanticized memories of the long-dead.

3. Overall, do you think the man tries to encourage or discourage his son to hope? Which does he do more? Is this a contradiction?

   Time: 7-10 minutes

   Discussion: At times, the man encourages his son to hope: he tells stories of the old world, tells him that "good guys" exist and that there may be other children out there. He maintains that neither of them will die. But at times, he does the opposite: he insists that there are no crows, that it is unlikely that they will meet a "good guy" and later, that the boat's former inhabitants are dead. The man is torn between wanting to give his son a happy, hopeful life and wanting to keep him safe from disillusionment. What results is a building-up and tearing-down of expectations that the boy must learn to balance.

4. Why do you think the boy throws his flute away?

   Time: 5 minutes

   Discussion: There is no definite, textual answer to this question. Students may speculate that this gesture could indicate the boy's disillusionment and his desire to not be seen as childish. The flute served no survival purpose--its sole value was entertainment. The boy never sees his father engaging in recreation, so it is likely that he decides non-essential items like the flute are unnecessary, and might even indicate weakness in comparison to his father's constant vigilance.

5. Who do you think Ely is, and why is he included in the story?

   Time: 7-10 minutes

   Discussion: Ely's name is likely a reference to the biblical prophet Eli. Ely demonstrates some suitably mystical qualities: his mysterious ability to survive, his advanced age, and his cryptic manner of speech. In fact, the man wonders if Ely might be a god in disguise. However, Ely takes the boy's charity and gives nothing in return. Despite Ely's manner, he often does not act prophetic, proclaiming the non-existence of god. It is likely that Ely stands for the corrupted and abandoned religious ideals of old, no longer relevant after the apocalypse.

Day 3 - Short Answer Quiz

1. How would you characterize the main characters' goals--are they short-term or long-term?

2. The boy asks the man why they couldn't help the people trapped in the farmhouse basement. What reason does the man give?

3. Where does the boy hope a crow would be able to fly to?

4. The man says in this section that, without food, he and the boy have ____ days until death.

5. As the boy sits in front of the stove in the bunker, he says to his father, "___ at last".

6. On the road, the man and the boy meet an old traveler. He says that his name is ____.

7. The boy is conflicted about taking food from the bunker. How does the man justify it?

____

8. To what creature does the man sometimes compare his son?

____

9. What happens to the boy's flute?

____

10. The man asks Ely how long he has been on the road. How does Ely respond?

____

Short Answer Quiz Key

1. Short-term.
2. The man says that they would risk being eaten by the cannibals if they helped.
3. Mars.
4. 10.
5. Warm.
6. Ely.
7. Acceptable answers:

   The people who stockpiled the food are dead.

   The people who stockpiled the food were "good guys," and would want them to have it.
8. An alien.
9. He throws it away.
10. Ely says that he has always been on the road.

Day 3 - Crossword Puzzle

ACROSS

2. The man finds stores of canned goods in this underground ______.
7. Luxurious; rich.
9. A framework on which climbing plants may grow.
12. The man dropped this in the cannibals' cellar.
13. "This is what the _____ guys do. They keep trying."
16. A semi-transparent screen.
17. The old man they meet on the road.
18. To set up temporary camp in an unsheltered area.
19. They find these growing on a farm.
20. Very cold.

DOWN

1. The boy wonders if there may be people alive on this planet.
3. A South African gold coin.
4. "________ at last."
5. A small room where people may leave their coat and shoes.
6. The boy asks if they have "long-term ________."
8. The man predicts they can go this many days before dying of starvation.
10. Without a will.
11. Cautious; wary.
14. Decaying organic matter on a forest floor.
15. "As the ______ flies."

Crossword Puzzle Answer Key

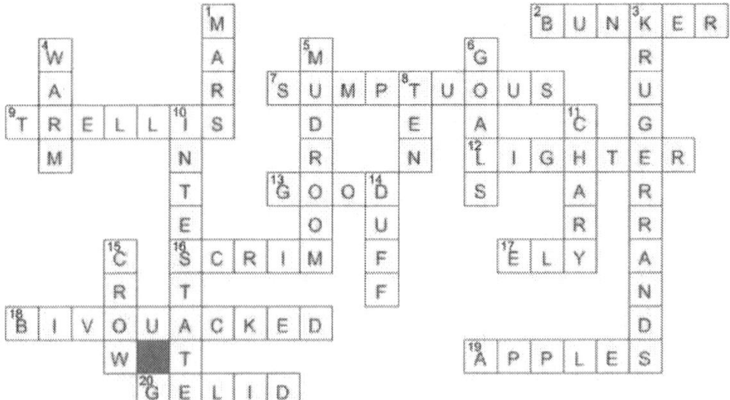

ACROSS

2. The man finds stores of canned goods in this underground ______.
7. Luxurious; rich.
9. A framework on which climbing plants may grow.
12. The man dropped this in the cannibals' cellar.
13. "This is what the _____ guys do. They keep trying."
16. A semi-transparent screen.
17. The old man they meet on the road.
18. To set up temporary camp in an unsheltered area.
19. They find these growing on a farm.
20. Very cold.

DOWN

1. The boy wonders if there may be people alive on this planet.
3. A South African gold coin.
4. "______ at last."
5. A small room where people may leave their coat and shoes.
6. The boy asks if they have "long-term ______."
8. The man predicts they can go this many days before dying of starvation.
10. Without a will.
11. Cautious; wary.
14. Decaying organic matter on a forest floor.
15. "As the ______ flies."

Day 3 - Vocabulary Quiz

Terms	Answers
1. ____ Chary	A. Very cold.
2. ____ Duff	B. To set up temporary camp in an unsheltered area.
3. ____ Trellis	C. Without a will.
4. ____ Mudroom	D. Cautious; wary.
5. ____ Intestate	E. A semi-transparent screen.
6. ____ Gelid	F. A South African gold coin.
7. ____ Krugerrand	G. A framework on which climbing plants may grow.
8. ____ Sumptuous	H. A small room adjacent to a home's entrance where people may leave their coat and shoes.
9. ____ Scrim	I. Luxurious; rich.
10. ____ Bivouac	J. Decaying organic matter on a forest floor.

Vocabulary Quiz Answer Key

1. D
2. J
3. G
4. H
5. C
6. A
7. F
8. I
9. E
10. B

Day 3 - Classroom Activities

1. The Ends of the World

Kind of Activity: Long-term Project
Objective: Trace the role of the apocalypse in literature and myth.
Common Core State Standards: CCSS.ELA-Literacy.CCRA.R.9; CCSS.ELA-Literacy.CCRA.W.10
Time: 30 minutes

Structure:

Introduce the concept of apocalypse and Endtimes in literature and religious writing. Have students identify apocalyptic narratives that are familiar to them. They can be from any medium: books, movies, television shows, video games, etc. Once you have made a list on the board or a large sheet of paper, try to make connections between the stories. Look for recurring plot elements and tropes. It may be helpful to make a chart or diagram in order to connect the texts visually.

Ask the class where they think apocalyptic stories come from. Identify the earliest apocalyptic stories as those of mythological or spiritual destruction: for example, the great flood in the ancient Mesopotamian Epic of Gilgamesh, or the Biblical flood. What do these stories have in common? Compare and contrast them with modern apocalyptic stories.

Finally, compare *The Road* to both mythological apocalyptic narratives and other contemporary ones. Identify the tropes and archetypes of the genre that *The Road* draws upon. As the unit continues, ask students to keep a reading journal and take note when a familiar trope of apocalyptic narrative occurs. Can you trace it back to the style of classical mythological/religious apocalypses, or is it unique to contemporary scientific/environmental apocalypses? What is the role of that particular trope in this context? What other ideas/images/motifs could have been used, and how would that change the text?

Ideans for Differentiated Instruction:

-Provide examples of both mythological apocalypse narratives and contemporary fictional ones.

-For students who need more guidance, provide scaffolding questions, visual organizers, and other prompting tools for use in their reading journals.

Assessment Ideas:

-Have students turn in their reading journals, either submitting individual response papers for each section of the text, or submitting one large journal at the end of the unit.

-Have students exchange journal entries and comment on one another's responses.

2. Comparative Literature Exercise: Byron's "Darkness"

Kind of Activity: Group Work
Objective: To identify recurrent apocalyptic archetypes in *The Road* and discuss their significance.
Common Core State Standards: CCSS.ELA-Literacy.CCRA.R.9; CCSS.ELA-Literacy.CCRA.L.5
Time: 30 minutes

Structure:

Print a copy of the poem "Darkness" by Lord George Gordon Byron for each student to read and annotate. This poem is a very early example of a literary apocalyptic narrative. It has many thematic and stylistic elements in common with the novel, and may have been one of McCarthy's influences. In "Darkness," as in *The Road*, it is the actions of humanity after the cataclysm that bring about the most horrifying destruction, not the cataclysm itself. Have students individually read and annotate their copies of the poem, looking specifically for similarities between the two texts.

Then, divide students into small groups, in which they can share their discoveries. Have each group work together to answer the following questions:

1.) How do the events described in "Darkness" remind you of *The Road*?

2.) How does the language or style of "Darkness" compare to that of *The Road*?

3.) Are the people in "Darkness" to blame for the end of the world? What about the people in *The Road*?

4.) What general statement do you think Byron is trying to make about humanity?

5.) Why do you think Byron chose to make this statement in the form of an apocalypse narrative?

After each group has finished composing an answer to each question, have them present their findings to the class. Ask students why they think certain archetypes, (such as civilized people devolving into savages and/or cannibals, fire, empty oceans, etc.) are so recurrent. What makes them relevant?

Ideans for Differentiated Instruction:

-Assign groups by varied skill level, so that more advanced students can help those who might have trouble with Byron's language.

-Assign roles within the groups based on strengths: a good note-taker might be a group scribe, while one who is comfortable speaking in large groups might present findings to the class as a whole.

-Consider providing an audio recording of the poem for students who would prefer listening to reading.

Assessment Ideas:

-Have a representative from each group take notes on their discussion and submit them to the instructor.

-Observe the students' contributions to the group discussion to evaluate their understanding of the text and issues being considered.

Day 4 - Reading Assignment

Students should read from page 174 - page to page 220.

Common Core Objectives

- CCSS.ELA-Literacy.CCRA.R.3 Analyze how and why individuals, events, or ideas develop and interact over the course of a text.
- CCSS.ELA-Literacy.CCRA.R.4 Interpret words and phrases as they are used in a text, including determining technical, connotative, and figurative meanings, and analyze how specific word choices shape meaning or tone.

Note that it is perfectly fine to expand any day's work into two days depending on the characteristics of the class, particularly if the class will engage in all of the suggested classroom exercises and activities and discuss all of the thought questions.

Content Summary for Teachers

Pages 174 - 220:

The man and the boy cross the coastal plains. The man's health is failing--he has gotten sicker and is beginning to cough up blood--but he tries to hide it from the boy. They find a long-abandoned train in the woods.

It takes them longer than expected to reach the coast, and the carnage they witness along the road grows increasingly disturbing and brutal. The boy sees the remains of a cooked human baby on a spit; he is traumatized and refuses to speak for days.

They find another house, raid its pantry for canned food, and make a fire in the fireplace. They stay for four days and recover somewhat before setting out for the coast again. They reach the sea shore, but it is a horrible disappointment. It is cold and grey, and smells of iodine. The boy plays in the water anyway.

Thought Questions (students consider while they read)

1. According to the man, there are other "good guys," but they are hiding from each other. What are the consequences of this way of thinking?
2. What does the man mean when he tells the boy, "What you put in your head is there forever"?
3. Earlier in the book, the man's memories are happy ones of the wilderness and his family. What kinds of memories does he recount in this section of the book? What might this change indicate?

4. The man tells the boy: "When your dreams are of some world that never was or of some world that never will be and you are happy again then you will have given up." Is this different from what the man has told his son in the beginning of the novel? What do you think of this philosophy?
5. Why does it matter that the sea isn't blue, and is "cold, desolate and birdless"?

Vocabulary (in order of appearance)

Page 177:

- Midden: A trash heap.
- Clapboards: Long, flat pieces of wood used for the siding on buildings.
- Kudzu: A climbing vine known for its rapid growth. An invasive species in the United States.
- Gullied: Filled with trenches or channels.

Page 180:

- Patterans: Coded signs left from one traveling Roma person (also called "gypsies") to another.
- Cairn: A pile of stones, usually constructed as a memorial.

Page 181:

- Commissary: A store in a prison or military base that sells food and basic provisions.

Page 184:

- Sundries: Assorted small items.
- Notions: Small useful items, often related to sewing.
- Dessicated: Completely without moisture; dried-out.

Page 188:

- Caustic: Corrosive.
- Bolus: A round mass or clod.

Page 200:

- Slough: Swampland.

Page 207:

- Lintel: The horizontal beam above a window or door.

Page 213:

- Disinter: To unbury something that has been deliberately buried.

Additional Homework

1. Search an academic database, like JSTOR.org or Google Scholar, for papers about *The Road*. Find one that interests you and compose a paragraph summarizing and explaining its thesis. Do you agree with the author's analysis?

Day 4 - Discussion of Thought Questions

1. According to the man, there are other "good guys," but they are hiding from each other. What are the consequences of this way of thinking?

   Time: 7-10 minutes

   Discussion: This indicates the man's awareness of the self-defeating nature of his own isolationism. He refuses to trust and is reluctant to communicate with anyone he meets on the road, especially if he encounters a group of people. This is eminently practical, and protects the man and the boy from "bad guys" who are dangerous. However, it also cuts them off from potential companions.

2. What does the man mean when he tells the boy, "What you put in your head is there forever"?

   Time: 5 minutes

   Discussion: The man wants to protect the boy from seeing atrocities that will traumatize him. Unfortunately, the boy is growing up in a world where protection from trauma is impossible: the land is littered with corpses, starvation is a daily struggle, and anyone you meet could be a violent cannibal. The man tries to shield his son from these realities for as long as possible, hoping that if the boy does not physically view the atrocities, they will not traumatize him.

3. Earlier in the book, the man's memories are happy ones of the wilderness and his family. What kinds of memories does he recount in this section of the book? What might this change indicate?

   Time: 7-10 minutes

   Discussion: As the man loses hope, he can't help but remember darker aspects of his childhood, because the happier memories cause too much pain. It may be perversely comforting for the man to think of, for instance, the disinterred cholera victims and the burning snakes, because these memories remind him that there were terrible things before the apocalypse as well. It puts the atrocities he witnesses into a slightly different, perhaps more bearable, context.

4. The man tells the boy: "When your dreams are of some world that never was or of some world that never will be and you are happy again then you will have given up." Is this different from what the man has told his son in the beginning of the novel? What do you think of this philosophy?

   Time: 7-10 minutes

   Discussion: Here, the man is encouraging his son not to look to stories of the past (or idealized stories of the future) for hope, because to do so means you are giving up on trying to improve your life as it is. This is a change from the man's approach at the beginning of the novel, when he tried to bolster the boy's spirits by telling him stories of the past. At first glance, this quote may appear quite dark and somewhat fatalistic, as if it means that allowing one's self to be happy is giving up. However, the quote does not preclude happiness, only happiness derived from impossible ideals.

5. Why does it matter that the sea isn't blue, and is "cold, desolate and birdless"?

   Time: 5-7 minutes

   Discussion: The man has often told his son about his pre-apocalypse memories of the ocean, in order to keep up the boy's morale. When they arrive, however, the ocean is grey, cold and dangerous. To the man, it is yet another childhood memory that has been twisted and corrupted by the post-apocalyptic world. To the boy, it is yet another hopeful illusion shattered. Arrival at the sea serves as a point of crucial disillusionment for both characters.

Day 4 - Short Answer Quiz

1. What does the boy find hidden in the woods?

2. When does the boy briefly stop talking to his father?

3. What do they find underneath a cake bell in an old-fashioned drugstore?

4. The man says: "When your dreams are of some world that never was or of some world that never will be and you are happy again then you will have _____ ____."

5. The man is concerned that the boy might never speak again after they see __________.

6. What does the man find buried in a field?

7. What is disappointing about the ocean?

8. What does the man say might be on the other side of the ocean?

9. Name one of the unhappy memories the man recalls from his childhood.

10. Why do the man and the boy have to cook the canned food they find?

Short Answer Quiz Key

1. A train.
2. After they leave Ely behind.
3. A human head.
4. Given up.
5. A human infant on a spit.
6. A Spanish coin.
7. It is not blue, it smells of iodine, and there are no birds.
8. Another father and his little boy.
9. Possible answers: he remembers watching some men set a den of snakes on fire; he remembers cholera victims being disinterred.
10. These particular foods are home-canned, not from a factory, and the man does not know if they have been contaminated by the poison in the atmosphere after the apocalyptic event.

Day 4 - Crossword Puzzle

ACROSS

3. Corrosive.
7. Long, flat pieces of wood used for the siding on buildings.
8. Filled with trenches or channels.
12. A store in a prison or military base that sells basic provisions.
14. The ocean smells like this.
15. A round mass or clod.
17. The boy finds this in the woods.
18. Victims of this disease were disinterred in the man's youth.
19. The boy is traumatized by seeing a cooked human ______.
20. Assorted small items.

DOWN

1. A climbing vine known for its rapid growth.
2. The horizontal beam above a window or door.
4. A pile of stones, usually constructed as a memorial.
5. They discover that the ocean is not this color.
6. To unbury something that has been deliberately buried.
9. Completely without moisture; dried-out.
10. Coded signs left from one gypsy to another.
11. The man finds this buried in a field.
13. A trash heap.
16. Swampland.

Crossword Puzzle Answer Key

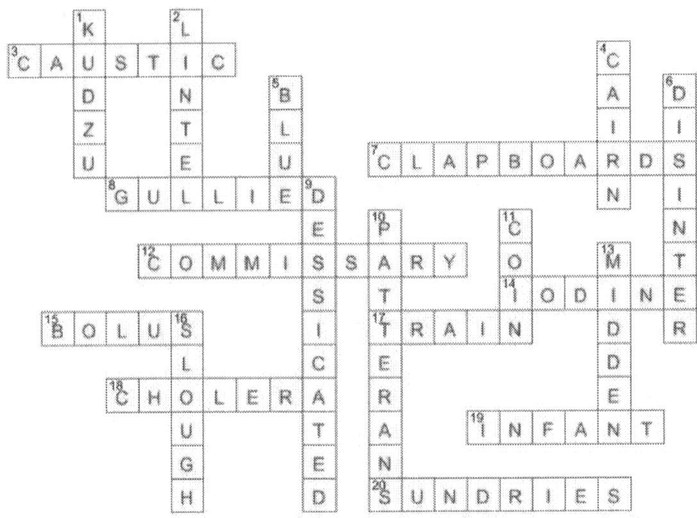

ACROSS

3. Corrosive.
7. Long, flat pieces of wood used for the siding on buildings.
8. Filled with trenches or channels.
12. A store in a prison or military base that sells basic provisions.
14. The ocean smells like this.
15. A round mass or clod.
17. The boy finds this in the woods.
18. Victims of this disease were disinterred in the man's youth.
19. The boy is traumatized by seeing a cooked human ______.
20. Assorted small items.

DOWN

1. A climbing vine known for its rapid growth.
2. The horizontal beam above a window or door.
4. A pile of stones, usually constructed as a memorial.
5. They discover that the ocean is not this color.
6. To unbury something that has been deliberately buried.
9. Completely without moisture; dried-out.
10. Coded signs left from one gypsy to another.
11. The man finds this buried in a field.
13. A trash heap.
16. Swampland.

Day 4 - Vocabulary Quiz

Terms

1. ____ Midden
2. ____ Clapboards
3. ____ Kudzu
4. ____ Gullied
5. ____ Patterans
6. ____ Cairn
7. ____ Commissary
8. ____ Sundries
9. ____ Notions
10. ____ Dessicated
11. ____ Caustic
12. ____ Bolus
13. ____ Slough
14. ____ Lintel
15. ____ Disinter

Answers

A. Coded signs left from one gypsy to another.

B. A climbing vine known for its rapid growth. An invasive species in the United States.

C. A round mass or clod.

D. Filled with trenches or channels.

E. Completely without moisture; dried-out.

F. Assorted small items.

G. Swampland.

H. To unbury something that has been deliberately buried.

I. Small useful items, often related to sewing.

J. Corrosive.

K. A pile of stones, usually constructed as a memorial.

L. A store in a prison or military base that sells food and basic provisions.

M. The horizontal beam above a window or door.

N. A trash heap.

O. Long, flat pieces of wood used for the siding on buildings.

Vocabulary Quiz Answer Key

1. N
2. O
3. B
4. D
5. A
6. K
7. L
8. F
9. I
10. E
11. J
12. C
13. G
14. M
15. H

Day 4 - Classroom Activities

1. The Man's Morality

   Kind of Activity: Role Play
   Objective: Examine some of the man's questionable actions from different perspectives.
   Common Core State Standards: CCSS.ELA-Literacy.CCRA.R.3
   Time: 30 minutes

   Structure:

   Begin a discussion about the man's moral compass. Ask the students to identify some actions of the man's that they find morally questionable (for example, abandoning Ely, and later stripping the man who tries to steal their cart on the beach). Make a list of some of these incidents.

   Next, have students choose partners and ask each pair to choose a morally questionable decision that the man has made. One student should take the role of the boy, arguing against the man's decision; the other should take the role of the man, arguing in favor of it. Students should role-play for at least five minutes. Then, have them switch roles and argue for the opposite side. Encourage students to try to debate "in character"--in other words, to make the argument they think their character would make, and not the argument they themselves would make.

   Afterwards, discuss the activity as a class. Ask how students felt initially regarding the man's morality, and if this activity has altered or reinforced their original opinions. As the book progresses, do they feel that the man's actions become less and less defensible? How about his ability to empathize? Does continued survival justify some actions? Any actions? Where should we draw the line? What is the difference between the man's sense of right and wrong and the boy's sense of right and wrong?

   Ideans for Differentiated Instruction:

   -Offer students the option of organizing their thoughts into charts or diagrams, if they are visual thinkers.

   -Provide examples of possible arguments for either side, as a prompt for students.

   Assessment Ideas:

   -Have one student from each pair act as the scribe, taking notes during the activity and submitting them to the instructor.

-Walk around among the groups during the activity to listen in on their discussions and offer feedback.

2. Obscure Word Bingo

Kind of Activity: Mixed Media
Objective: Learn about some of the esoteric vocabulary that Cormac McCarthy uses in The Road.
Common Core State Standards: CCSS.ELA-Literacy.CCRA.L.4; CCSS.ELA-Literacy.CCRA.R.4
Time: 30 minutes

Structure:

Discuss the author's use of unfamiliar words in *The Road*. Ask students if they find the vocabulary confusing or distracting. Ask why students think McCarthy chooses to use these words, particularly the archaic ones. For example, the word "salitter" is no longer in the dictionary, but has been traced to the works of Jakob Boehme, a 17th century Christian mystic. Discuss how precise the meanings of many of these obscure terms are, noting that McCarthy tries to be as specific in his descriptions as possible. You may want to suggest to students that McCarthy's language itself reflects a major theme in *The Road*: how beautiful things can become forgotten or irrelevant with time.

As a class, come up with a list of 25 vocabulary words from the text that stand out to students as obscure or archaic. Have each student make a bingo sheet on a piece of paper (five spaces across by five spaces down, with a free space in the center). Students should pick words from the vocabulary list, and write them in random spaces on their sheet of paper. Read out the definitions to these words at random. If a student calls out the correct word, they may cross it off on their bingo sheet. The first student to cross off five in a row wins, but you can keep playing until all the words have been defined.

Ideans for Differentiated Instruction:

-Consider allowing students to pair up and work from the same bingo board, so that they can help one another.

-Provide clues based on word roots or similar words in other languages, if applicable.

Assessment Ideas:

-Evaluate students' contributions to the discussion before the bingo game, and their participation during the game.

-Have students turn in their bingo boards and any notes they have made during the activity.

Day 5 - Reading Assignment

Students should read page 220 to the end.

Common Core Objectives

- CCSS.ELA-Literacy.RL.9-10.7 Analyze the representation of a subject or a key scene in two different artistic mediums, including what is emphasized or absent in each treatment (e.g., Auden's "Musée des Beaux Arts" and Breughel's Landscape with the Fall of Icarus).
- CCSS.ELA-Literacy.CCRA.R.2 Determine central ideas or themes of a text and analyze their development; summarize the key supporting details and ideas.

Note that it is perfectly fine to expand any day's work into two days depending on the characteristics of the class, particularly if the class will engage in all of the suggested classroom exercises and activities and discuss all of the thought questions.

Content Summary for Teachers

Pages 220 to end:

The man investigates a sailboat, and finds a few useful items and some food. The boy forgets the pistol on the beach, and the two have a brief panic that it will be lost or stolen, but they find it unharmed. Now they must find their way back to the campsite through the darkness and rain, though.

The man finds a flarepistol and the two fire it off in a brief moment of excitement. The boy realizes, however, that "good guys" will never be able to see the flare because of all the ash obscuring the sky. After this, he abruptly becomes very ill and develops a fever. The man stays by his side and cares for him constantly, terrified that his son will die. The boy recovers, but the man is still filled with fear.

The two have a brief scare when a vagabond tries to steal the cart of supplies, but he is weak and the man frightens him away - but not before insisting he strip and leaving him helpless and humiliated. The boy is horrified.

They don't travel much farther before the man is shot with an arrow and wounded. Soon he is unable to travel, and tells the boy to keep "carrying the fire" and to continue without him. The boy stays with his father until he dies, and then comes across an unexpected surprise: a kind stranger, with a family and two children, who is more than willing to care for the boy. The boy buries his father, but promises to always preserve his memory and talk to him.

The book closes with a description of the ancient but long-dead brook trout in mountain streams.

Thought Questions (students consider while they read)

1. Before the man dies, the boy is hopeless and depressed. He sees little point in life. What might change his mind after the man dies?
2. Why do you think the boy prefers talking to his father over talking to God?
3. Discuss the following exchange between the man and the boy.

   "*Do you want me to tell you a story?*

   No.

   Why not?

   The boy looked at him and looked away.

   Why not?

   Those stories are not true.

   They dont have to be true.

   They're stories.

   Yes.

   But in the stories we're always helping people and we dont help people."
4. Do you consider the book's ending to be happy? Why or why not?
5. Examine the final paragraph of the book. Why do you think it was included?

Vocabulary (in order of appearance)

Page 222:

- Sepulchre: A tomb or grave.
- Stanchion: An upright support.

Page 225:

- Clerestory: High windows that are above eye level, usually to let in light.

Page 227:

- Humidor: An airtight container for storing cigars and cigarettes at a constant humidity level.
- Sextant: A navigational instrument.

Page 249:

- Travois: A sled used for porting goods.

Page 261:

- Cognate: Relation.
- Salitter: The essence of God.
- Dolmen: A type of ancient tomb.

Page 262:

- Bollard: A short post to which a ship may be secured by rope.

Page 274:

- Hydroptic: Thirsty.

Page 280:

- Loess: A sediment formed by wind.
- Mortified: Unhealthy; crumbling.

Page 286:

- Wimple: To ripple or wave.

Page 287:

- Torsional: Related to twisting.
- Vermiculate: Covered in intricate, wavy lines.

Additional Homework

1. Make a diagram or other visual representation of the character arcs of the man and the boy. Include key events for each, and identify where you think each experienced changes in their beliefs, behavior or outlook.

Day 5 - Discussion of Thought Questions

1. Before the man dies, the boy is hopeless and depressed. He sees little point in life. What might change his mind after the man dies?

   Time: 5-7 minutes

   Discussion: The boy understands that he is responsible for "carrying the fire" now that the man has died. He also encounters a new family with children of their own. This makes the boy feel that there is hope, for both himself and the future of the earth.

2. Why do you think the boy prefers talking to his father over talking to God?

   Time: 5-7 minutes

   Discussion: Students may have noticed the religious undertones in the text, particularly in the relationship between the man and the boy. In several instances, the man refers to his son as a god, endowing him with divine qualities of purity and goodness. After the man's death, these roles reverse. Students should be encouraged to compare this to the concept of God as a father as it appears in Judeo-Christian belief systems.

3. Discuss the following exchange between the man and the boy.

   "*Do you want me to tell you a story?*

   No.

   Why not?

   The boy looked at him and looked away.

   Why not?

Those stories are not true.

They dont have to be true.

They're stories.

Yes.

But in the stories we're always helping people and we dont help people."

Time: 5-7 minutes

Discussion: You may want to touch upon what this reveals about the shifting characterizations of the man and the boy. It is also a good moment to discuss the importance of storytelling, for the characters: what do their stories reflect? Why does the man only tell happy stories? What would the boy prefer? Etc.

4. Do you consider the book's ending to be happy? Why or why not?

   Time: 5-7 minutes

   Discussion: Students might note that the family the boy encounters appears to be well-meaning in taking him in. However, it is not at all clear that they are definitely good--they could have ulterior motives. The ending is thus fairly ambiguous, although it might be of comfort to some readers that the boy is able to go on after his father's death, and is willing to trust people after all he has been through.

5. Examine the final paragraph of the book. Why do you think it was included?

   Time: 7-10 minutes

Discussion: This paragraph is a brief glance at the beauty that has gone out of the world in which *The Road* is set. It is juxtaposed against the descriptions of ashen wasteland that have dominated the book until this point, and reminds the reader what inhabitants of the post-apocalyptic world are missing out on. It might be interpreted as a final warning, encouraging readers to appreciate and preserve the wonder of the natural world. McCarthy treats this scene with almost spiritual resonance.

Day 5 - Short Answer Quiz

1. What does the sea smell like?

____

2. What do the man and the boy discover abandoned on the beach?

____

3. What does the man find in a square oak box with dovetailed corners?

____

4. What does the boy forget on the beach?

____

5. Who shoots the flaregun?

____

6. Shortly after they shoot off the flare, what happens to the boy?

____

7. How is the man injured?

____

8. When the son worries about the other little boy across the ocean, how does the man reassure him?

____

9. Who does the boy talk to instead of god?

____

10. What animal is described in the book's final passage?

____

Short Answer Quiz Key

1. Iodine.
2. A ship.
3. A sextant.
4. The pistol.
5. The man.
6. He gets sick. "He develops a fever" is also an acceptable answer.
7. He is shot with an arrow.
8. He says that Goodness will find the little boy.
9. His father.
10. Brook trout.

Day 5 - Crossword Puzzle

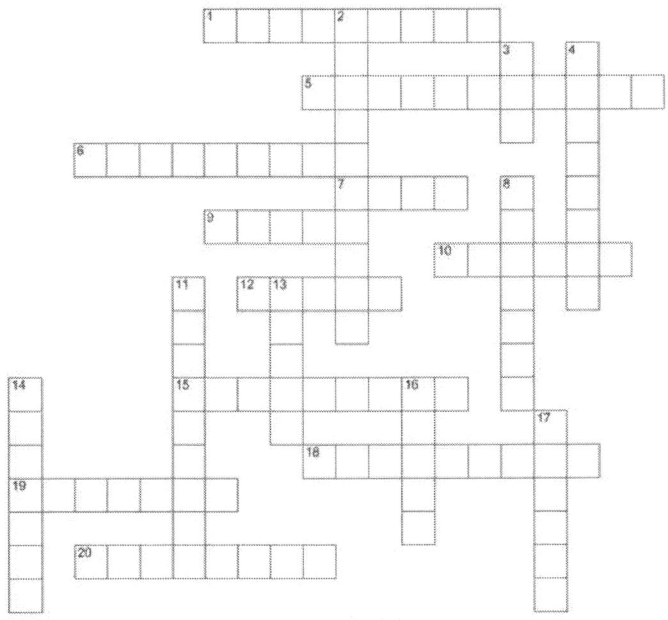

ACROSS

1. An upright support.
5. Covered in intricate, wavy lines.
6. A tomb or grave.
7. The man discovers this abandoned on the beach.
9. The animals in the book's final passage.
10. A type of ancient tomb.
12. The man shoots this into the sky.
15. Twisting.
18. Thirsty.
19. A sled used for porting goods.
20. "_____ will find the little boy."

DOWN

2. High windows that are above eye level, usually to let in light.
3. The boy accidentally leaves this behind.
4. The essence of God.
8. A short post to which a ship may be secured by rope.
11. Unhealthy; crumbling.
13. A sediment formed by wind.
14. A navigational tool that the man finds.
16. What the man is shot with.
17. To ripple or wave.

Crossword Puzzle Answer Key

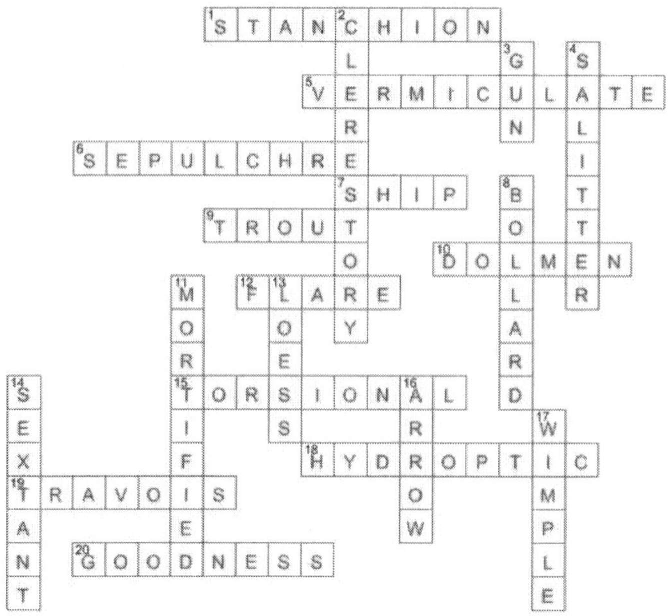

ACROSS

1. An upright support.
5. Covered in intricate, wavy lines.
6. A tomb or grave.
7. The man discovers this abandoned on the beach.
9. The animals in the book's final passage.
10. A type of ancient tomb.
12. The man shoots this into the sky.
15. Twisting.
18. Thirsty.
19. A sled used for porting goods.
20. "_____ will find the little boy."

DOWN

2. High windows that are above eye level, usually to let in light.
3. The boy accidentally leaves this behind.
4. The essence of God.
8. A short post to which a ship may be secured by rope.
11. Unhealthy; crumbling.
13. A sediment formed by wind.
14. A navigational tool that the man finds.
16. What the man is shot with.
17. To ripple or wave.

Day 5 - Vocabulary Quiz

Terms

1. ____ Sepulchre
2. ____ Stanchion
3. ____ Clerestory
4. ____ Humidor
5. ____ Sextant
6. ____ Travois
7. ____ Cognate
8. ____ Salitter
9. ____ Dolmen
10. ____ Bollard
11. ____ Hydroptic
12. ____ Loess
13. ____ Mortified
14. ____ Wimple
15. ____ Torsional
16. ____ Vermiculate

Answers

A. A type of ancient tomb.
B. Unhealthy; crumbling.
C. To ripple or wave.
D. A sled used for porting goods.
E. The essence of God.
F. An upright support.
G. A short post to which a ship may be secured by rope.
H. A sediment formed by wind.
I. High windows that are above eye level, usually to let in light.
J. Thirsty.
K. Related to twisting.
L. An airtight container for storing cigars and cigarettes at a constant humidity level.
M. A navigational instrument.
N. Covered in intricate, wavy lines.
O. Relation.
P. A tomb or grave.

Vocabulary Quiz Answer Key

1. P
2. F
3. I
4. L
5. M
6. D
7. O
8. E
9. A
10. G
11. J
12. H
13. B
14. C
15. K
16. N

Day 5 - Classroom Activities

1. Film Adaptation

Kind of Activity: Classwide Discussion
Objective: Watch the 2009 film adaptation of *The Road* and compare it to the text.
Common Core State Standards: CCSS.ELA-Literacy.CCRA.R.7
Time: Length of film plus an additional 20 minutes

Structure:

As a class, watch the 2009 film adaptation of *The Road*. When you have finished, students discuss the following questions:

- Did seeing the characters portrayed make them easier to relate to? Why or why not?

- Were the scenes of destruction as you imagined them?

- Did you find the character interactions more sentimental in the book or the film? Why?

- Compare the ending of the film to the ending of the book. Did you find one more effective or believable? Which one and why?

Finally, discuss whether you feel the film is a successful adaptation of the novel.

Ideans for Differentiated Instruction:

-Provide students with scaffolding questions or visual organizers to take notes during the movie.

-Encourage students to skim the novel as they watch the film, to reinforce connections between them and note where they diverge.

Assessment Ideas:
Have students write a review of the film assessing its success or failure as an adaptation of the book. They may want to read the reviews (published critical reviews only, not fan reviews) on critic aggregator websites like Rottentomatoes.com.

2. Alternate Ending

Kind of Activity: Individual Writing
Objective: Apply what you have learned about the themes of The Road and write your own alternate ending (or epilogue) to the novel
Common Core State Standards: CCSS.ELA-Literacy.CCRA.R.2
Time: 40 minutes.

Structure:

Discuss the end of The Road; the scene in which the boy is adopted into a new family. Ask students the following questions:

- Did you find the scene satisfying? Was it believable?

- Did you feel it was out of place with the rest of the book?

- Did it change your mind about some of the man's paranoid behavior?

Some students may have thought that the book's relatively happy ending seemed unrealistic based on what they already knew about the world in which The Road is set. It is worth taking into consideration, however, that the boy and the man may have encountered trustworthy people in their travels and were simply too cautious to make contact. Even within the novel, not everyone they come across is a confirmed threat. It is possible that their self-imposed isolation was unnecessary all along. Discuss whether or not this was essential to their survival, and if students would have behaved differently.

Assign students to compose either an alternate ending or an epilogue to The Road. Students may have the option to either write an entirely new ending, or to write an extra chapter continuing from where the book left off. Encourage them to mimic McCarthy's prose as closely as possible. They should include a short, one to two page analysis of their story explaining how it confirms or alters what they feel to be the message of the book.

Assessment Ideas:
- Grade students on the short alternate ending they compose, as well as their written analysis of it.

Final Paper

Essay Questions

1. How does the boy provide possible redemption and hopefulness for the future of humanity?

2. Some critics have expressed concern about the way women are portrayed in *The Road*. Do you agree or disagree with the argument that the novel portrays women poorly?

3. Why do you think Cormac McCarthy chose not to give the characters names?

4. Do you think the man is right about the world being made up of "good guys" and "bad guys"? Why or why not?

5. What does "carrying the fire" mean, and why is it important?

Advice on research sources

Ask your librarian for books on the following topics:

* The hero's journey

* Post-apocalyptic fiction

* Myths

* Religious texts

* Survival

Grading rubric for essays

Style:

* words: spelling and diction

* sentences: grammar and punctuation

* paragraphs: organization

* essay: structure

* argument: rhetoric, reasonableness, creativity

Content:

* accuracy

* use of evidence -- at least two quotes

* addresses the question

* completeness

(* optional, based on prompt: uses literary concepts)

Final Paper Answer Key

Remember that essays about literature should not be graded with a cookie-cutter approach whereby specific words or ideas are required. See the grading rubric above for a variety of criteria to use in assessing answers to the essay questions. This answer key thus functions as a store of ideas for students who need additional guidance in framing their answers.

1. How does the boy provide possible redemption and hopefulness for the future of humanity?

   A strong response might focus on the development of the boy's moral code. Despite the horrific circumstances in which he has been raised, the boy remains kind, loving, and empathetic. While his father was bitter and trusted no one, the boy is capable of trust and empathy. He is also very well adapted to the hardships of survival, arguably better so than his father.

2. Some critics have expressed concern about the way women are portrayed in *The Road*. Do you agree or disagree with the argument that the novel portrays women poorly?

   An essay should identify the lack of female characters, and may describe the few who are mentioned: always pregnant or mothers or food. A strong essay should include an analysis of the man's dead wife. In a book where survival is the only goal, suicide may imply weakness of character. Students should pull evidence from the text to support this, and contrast the weak-willed and selfish wife to her perseverant and selfless (at least where his child is concerned) husband. Language alluding to her "infidelity" with death may also help to support a strong argument.

3. Why do you think Cormac McCarthy chose not to give the characters names?

   A strong essay response should address how the characters' namelessness allows them to be archetypal everyman figures onto which the reader may easily project him/herself. Additionally, their namelessness could be said to highlight the loss of identity that the apocalypse has thrust upon all humans, and the new irrelevance of many things that were once highly valued parts of the human experience.

4. Do you think the man is right about the world being made up of "good guys" and "bad guys"? Why or why not?

   A strong essay should address the problematic nature of this binary. Some students may say that the man was justified: since he feels he cannot trust anyone he encounters on the road, he must label them as bad guys, particularly to protect his son. Some students may argue that this is justified to keep his son safe, and to keep him from feeling guilt over violence done to strangers for survival.

However, the man creates a situation by which people can only be one or the other. This label can be used to justify any action he may take toward perceived "bad guys," and arguably contributes to the man's gradual moral decay. It could also risk damaging his son's capacity to empathize and connect.

5. What does "carrying the fire" mean, and why is it important?

   The man tells his son that they are "carrying the fire," which represents their adherence to the old values of righteousness and good. As "the fire" is not something physical, it is the one hope that can never disappoint the boy. As long as he remains true to what his father has taught him, he will always be able to carry the fire, which gives him purpose. In a world without electricity or mechanization, fire in the greatest source of power.

Final Exam

A. Multiple Choice

Circle the letter corresponding to the best answer.

1. Who is Ely?

   (A) A kind but intimidating young man.
   (B) A cannibal.
   (C) A mysterious, sickly old traveler.
   (D) The man's father.

2. What is approaching that the man wants to travel South to avoid?

   (A) Winter.
   (B) Starvation.
   (C) Radiation.
   (D) Earthquakes.

3. How do the man and the boy carry their supplies?

   (A) In a pack.
   (B) In a cart.
   (C) In a car.
   (D) In a van.

4. Fill in the blank: "If he is not the _______, then God never spoke."

   (A) Word of God.
   (B) Alien.
   (C) Messiah.
   (D) Boy.

5. When a stranger tries to steal their supplies, what does the man take from him?

   (A) His clothes.
   (B) His life.
   (C) His food.
   (D) Nothing.

6. Why does the man leave the pistol with the boy whenever they separate?

    (A) To defend the man.
    (B) To keep the gun safe.
    (C) To kill himself before others can.
    (D) To defend himself.

7. The father washes another man's _____ out of his son's hair.

    (A) Blood.
    (B) Vomit.
    (C) Bone.
    (D) Brains.

8. The man tells his son that they aren't dying of starvation because _________.

    (A) They are dying of sickness.
    (B) They'll freeze to death first.
    (C) Someone will rescue them.
    (D) It takes 10 days to die of starvation.

9. When the man says, "Can you do it? When the time comes?", what is "it"?

    (A) Kill the boy.
    (B) Kill himself.
    (C) Kill his wife.
    (D) Defend against cannibals.

10. What literary award did *The Road* win?

    (A) Booker Prize.
    (B) Pulitzer Prize.
    (C) Caldecott Award.
    (D) Nobel Prize.

11. What is the man shot with?

(A) A dart.
(B) A bullet.
(C) An arrow.
(D) A BB.

12. What does the boy draw on his face mask?

(A) Fangs.
(B) A dog.
(C) A smile.
(D) A frown.

13. When the boy says that he wishes he was with his mother, what does he mean?

(A) He wishes he did not have to travel.
(B) He wishes he was in the house where he used to live.
(C) He wishes he was dead.
(D) He wishes he was not with his father.

14. To whom is *The Road* dedicated?

(A) Cormac McCarthy's father.
(B) Cormac McCarthy's wife.
(C) No one.
(D) Cormac McCarthy's son.

15. What does the boy cover his father's corpse with?

(A) Dirt.
(B) Leaves.
(C) Blankets.
(D) A tarp.

16. Who does the boy primarily talk to after his father dies?

(A) The man.
(B) Good guys.
(C) God.
(D) His mother.

17. What is the man's sole reason for survival?

(A) His son.
(B) God.
(C) The fire.
(D) His wife.

18. Who or what does the boy hope he might find at the coast?

(A) Ely.
(B) His mother.
(C) Other children.
(D) A dog.

19. How does the boy's mother die?

(A) She starves to death.
(B) She kills herself with a sharp piece of obsidian.
(C) In childbirth.
(D) She shoots herself.

20. What one word does the boy often repeat to his father?

(A) Okay.
(B) Fine.
(C) Fire.
(D) No.

B. Short Answer

1. When the boy asks what the man has found in the bunker, what does the man say?

____

2. When was the boy born?

____

3. What does the last passage in the novel describe?

____

4. How can the reader tell that the man is sick?

____

5. How does the boy feel about the family he meets after his father dies?

____

6. What categories does the man divide people into?

____

7. What is the ocean like once the protagonists reach it?

____

8. Why is the boy's mother absent from this journey?

9. Do the readers ever learn the nature of the apocalyptic event?

10. What mementos do the man and the boy initially travel with?

C. Vocabulary

Terms

1. ____ Vestibular
2. ____ Discalced
3. ____ Claggy
4. ____ Viscera
5. ____ Chary
6. ____ Gelid
7. ____ Patterans
8. ____ Bolus
9. ____ Lintel
10. ____ Vermiculate

Answers

A. A round mass or clod.
B. Gummed up; sticky.
C. Cautious; wary.
D. Internal organs; guts.
E. Covered in intricate, wavy lines.
F. The horizontal beam above a window or door.
G. Barefoot
H. Coded signs left from one traveling Roma person (often called gypsies) to another.
I. Very cold.
J. Relating to one's sense of balance.

D. Short Essays

1. What role does faith play in *The Road*? Use examples from the text to support your

2. What is the man's wife's relationship with the idea of death?

3. What does the man consider to be "giving up," and how does he discourage his son from doing so?

Final Exam Answer Key

A. Multiple Choice Answer Key

1. C
2. A
3. B
4. A
5. A
6. C
7. D
8. D
9. A
10. B
11. C
12. A
13. C
14. D
15. C
16. A
17. A
18. C
19. B
20. A

B. Short Answer Key

1. "Everything." (A description of the bunker's contents is also acceptable. For example: canned food, a generator, clothes, etc.)
2. As the apocalyptic event was occurring.
3. Brook trout swimming in the mountains before the apocalypse.
4. He coughs up blood.
5. He is hopeful about them; they seem to be kind and welcoming.
6. Good guys and bad guys.
7. The ocean is grey, lifeless, and smells of chemicals.
8. She has committed suicide.
9. No.
10. The man carries a picture of his wife, and the boy carries some of his toys.

C. Vocabulary Answer Key

1. J
2. G
3. B
4. D
5. C
6. I
7. H
8. A
9. F
10. E

D. Short Essays Answer Key

1. There is religious imagery throughout the novel, such as the encounter with the mysterious vagrant Ely. The man compares the boy to a god on several occasions. In the end, the boy speaks seems to revere his father as a god-like figure after he has died. There is also the faith that the man encourages in his son: that there are other "good guys," that they will survive, that the ocean will be blue and beautiful, that their lives will improve. This faith keeps the boy's spirits up, despite his eventual disillusionment with the ocean and many other things. In the end, his faith in other people may be rewarded: the family he meets after his father's death appears to be kind and protective. However, this may be a deception and they could be out to harm him. That interpretation would significantly alter the ultimate message of the novel with regard to faith.
2. She thinks of death as an illicit lover. A particularly insightful response will explore the implications of this metaphor--the woman romanticizes death as an escape from the fear and depression of post-apocalyptic life, and she confesses that she has fallen in love with the idea of it. Essays should reinforce these ideas with examples from the text.
3. There are two things that the man considers to be "giving up": living in the past, and committing suicide. Living in the past allows one to avoid facing the present, particularly if circumstances are difficult and unpleasant. The man sees this as a kind of weakness, and a way of giving up on the present and future. Similarly, committing suicide is a way of giving up quite literally, but it is selfish and leaves loved ones to deal with reality on top of their grief. The man discourages his son from indulging in either of these

kinds of "giving up" or weakness. Strong responses should note how the man conveys these values to the boy, using textual examples.

Made in the USA
San Bernardino, CA
30 January 2019